MAX on life
cd-book :: study

Becoming a
Student
of God's Word

:: 4 Interactive Bible Studies
for Individuals or Small Groups

MAX LUCADO

THOMAS NELSON PUBLISHERS

CONTENTS

HOW TO USE
THIS STUDY GUIDE

Congratulations! You are making God's Word a priority. These moments of reflection will change you forever. Here are suggestions for you to get the most out of your individual study.

1

As you begin each study, pray that God will speak to you through His Word.

2

Read the overview to each study, then listen to the audio segment, taking notes on the worksheet provided.

3

Following the audio segment, respond to the personal Bible study and reflection questions. These questions are designed to take you deeper into God's Word and help you focus on God and on the theme of the study.

:: 4 ::

There are three types of questions used in the study. *Observation* questions focus on the basic facts: who, what, when, where, and how. *Interpretation* questions delve into the meaning of the passage. *Application* questions help you get practical: discovering the implications of the text for growing in Christ. These three keys will help you unlock the treasures of Scripture.

:: 5 ::

Write your answers to the questions in the spaces provided or in a personal journal. Writing brings clarity and deeper understanding of yourself and of God's Word.

:: 6 ::

Keep a Bible dictionary handy. Use it to look up any unfamiliar words, names, or places.

:: 7 ::

Have fun! Studying God's Word can bring tremendous rewards to your life. Allow the Holy Spirit to illuminate your mind to the amazing applications each study can have in your daily life. ■

INTRODUCTION

BECOMING A STUDENT
OF GOD'S WORD

To read the Bible is to stir questions of interpretation. For example: Jesus washed His disciples' feet. He commanded that His disciples do the same. We, however, have no foot-washing ceremony. . . should we?

"A woman must not wear men's clothing" (Deuteronomy 22:5). Does that mean women should sell their jeans?

Paul commanded Christians in Rome to greet one another with a holy kiss. Are we disobeying if we don't pucker up? If we are to kiss, where are we to kiss? How often should we kiss? What if we forget to kiss? Can someone kiss for us in our absence?

How do we answer questions such as these? We begin by remembering that the Bible is God's Word given in man's language. Scripture is a marriage of eternal truth with historical particularity.

- It was written in another time.
- It was written in another culture.
- It was written in another language.

Our world is different than the world of the Bible. Our language, dress, and culture are not the same of those of ancient Israel.

It is my hope that this study, *Becoming a Student of God's Word*, will provide you with the tools you need to better understand the Bible and apply it to your own life. ∎

*Do you know a book that you
are willing to put under your head
for a pillow when you lie dying?
That is the book you want
to study while you are living.
There is but one such book
in the world: The Bible.*

JOSEPH COOK

LESSON ONE:

A MOST PECULIAR BOOK

The grass withers and the flowers fall,
but the word of our God stands forever.

ISAIAH 40:8

OVERVIEW

The Bible is a peculiar book. Words crafted in another language. Deeds done in a distant era. Events recorded in a far-off land. Counsel offered to a foreign people. This is a peculiar book.

It's surprising that anyone reads it. It's too old. Some of its writings date back five thousand years. It's too bizarre. The book speaks of incredible floods, fires, earthquakes, and people with supernatural abilities. It's too radical. The Bible calls for undying devotion to a Carpenter who called Himself God's Son.

Logic says this book shouldn't survive. It's too old, too bizarre, too radical.

The Bible has been banned, burned, scoffed, and ridiculed. Scholars have mocked it as foolish. Kings have branded it as illegal. A thousand times over the grave has been dug and the dirge has begun, but somehow the Bible never stays in the grave. Not only has it survived, it has thrived. It is the single most popular book in all of history. It has been the best-selling book in the world for three hundred years!

There is no way on earth to explain it. Which perhaps is the only explanation. The answer? The Bible's durability is not found on earth; it is found in heaven. For the millions who have tested its claims and claimed its promises there is but one answer—the Bible is God's book and God's voice.

What is the purpose of the Bible? Salvation. God's highest passion is to get His children home. His book, the Bible, describes His plan of salvation. The purpose of the Bible is to proclaim God's plan and passion to save His children.

Before reading the Bible, pray. Invite God to speak to you. Don't go to Scripture looking for your idea; go searching for His. The Bible is not a newspaper to be skimmed, but rather a mine to be quarried.

Don't be discouraged if your reading reaps a small harvest. Some days a lesser portion is all that is needed. What is important is to search every day for that day's message. A steady diet of God's Word over a lifetime builds a healthy soul and mind.

A little girl returned from her first day at school. Her mother asked, "Did you learn anything today?" "Apparently not enough," the girl responded, "I have to go back tomorrow and the next day and the next...." Such is the case with learning. And such is the case with the study of God's Word. Understanding comes little by little over a lifetime.

Are you ready to roll up your sleeves and begin? Let's get started!

PART 1:
FOLLOW-ALONG NOTES

USE THIS WORKSHEET AS YOU LISTEN TO "HOW TO STUDY THE BIBLE, PART 1."

- The Word of God has endured for centuries.

- The Bible is a Book that records the history of God's involvement on earth.

- *Jesus traveled to Nazareth where He had grown up. On the Sabbath day He went to the synagogue as He always did and stood up to read. The book of Isaiah the prophet was given to Him.* Luke 4:16–17 NCV

- Book = Biblos = Bible

- The Bible is a collection of books with one central theme.

- The Bible is divided into two testaments or _____.

SECTIONS OF THE BIBLE

OLD TESTAMENT:

- The _____ Section: Genesis through Deuteronomy

- The _____ Section: Joshua through Esther

- The _____ Section: Job through Song of Solomon

- The _____ Section: Isaiah through Malachi

NEW TESTAMENT:

- The _____ Section: Matthew, Mark, Luke, John

- The _____ Section: Acts

- The _____ Section: Doctrinal Epistles

- The _____ Section: Revelation

KEY FACTS

- _____ writers wrote the Bible over a _____-century period.

- The OT was written in _____; the New Testament in _____.

- The central theme of the Bible: _____.

PART 2:
GOING DEEPER

PERSONAL STUDY AND REFLECTION

NOTE: SENTENCES IN ITALICS ARE DIRECTLY FROM MAX'S AUDIO LESSON.

- What is the purpose of the Bible? Let the Bible itself answer that question. According to 2 Timothy 3:15, what is the purpose of the Holy Scriptures?

_____

_____

- *This is the reason this book has endured through the centuries: It dares to tackle the toughest questions about life. But how do we use the Bible? Countless copies of Scripture sit unread on bookshelves and nightstands simply because people don't know how to read it. What can we do to make the Bible real in our lives? The clearest answer is found in the words of Jesus.*

According to Matthew 7:7, what three steps does Jesus say we should take to understand the Bible?

_____

_____

_____

- The first step to understanding the Bible is to ask God to help us. According to John 14:26, whose help should we ask for? What is promised to us in this passage?

_____

_____

• *Any worthy find requires effort. The Bible is no exception. To understand the Bible, you don't have to be brilliant, but you must be willing to roll up your sleeves and search. This is step two in understanding the Bible.*

Write out 2 Timothy 2:15. To you, what does it mean to "use the true teaching in the right way"?

_____

_____

_____

_____

_____

_____

_____

- *Here's a practical point. Study the Bible a bit at a time. Hunger is not satisfied by eating twenty-one meals in one sitting once a week. The body needs a steady diet to remain strong. So does the soul. When God sent food to His people in the wilderness, He didn't provide loaves already made.*

According to Exodus 16:14, how was the manna sent?

_____

_____

- God sends spiritual food the same way. He opens the heavens with just enough nutrients for today's hunger. How does Isaiah 28:10 tell us the Scriptures should be studied?

_____

_____

_____

_____

- *There is a third step to understanding the Bible. After the asking and seeking comes knocking. After you ask and search, then knock.*

What does Matthew 7:7 say will happen for the person who knocks?

_____

_____

- *To knock is to stand at God's door. To make yourself available. To climb the steps, cross the porch, stand at the doorway, and volunteer. Knocking goes beyond the realm of thinking and into the realm of acting.*

Summarize the three steps involved in understanding the Bible. How have you followed these three steps in your own Bible study? How can you follow them in the future?

_____

_____

_____

- It's one thing to know what to do. It's another thing to do it. But for those who do it, those who choose to obey, a special reward awaits them. What is this reward (see James 1:25)?

_____

_____

_____

What a promise! Happiness comes to those who do what they read! It's the same with medicine. If you only read the label but ignore the pills, it won't help. It's the same with food. If you only read the recipe but never cook, you won't be fed. And it's the same with the Bible. If you only read the words but never obey, you'll never know the joy God has promised.

Ask. Search. Knock. Simple, isn't it? Why don't you give it a try? If you do, you'll see why the Book you are holding is the most remarkable book in history. ■

*This Book will
keep you from sin,
or sin will keep you
from this Book.*

D. L. MOODY

LESSON TWO:

THE PURPOSE OF THE BIBLE

I have hidden your word
in my heart that I might
not sin against you.

PSALM 119:11

OVERVIEW

The roads of San Antonio, Texas, where I live, confuse me. When I think I'm going south, I see the sun and realize I'm headed west. When I think I'm going toward the city, I find that I am going away from the city. A sympathetic friend explained the winding roads to me by pointing out that the original streets were cattle trails.

So, to keep from getting lost, I bought a compass. The kind you can install in your car. It is round and has a floating arrow. I took it to my car with great expectations. Finally I would be oriented and have direction. But then I read the instructions: "Face compass north and adjust the arrow."

I shook my head. If I knew where north was, I wouldn't need a compass, I thought.

We are studying the compass of life—the Bible. Just like a compass, it serves as a tool of orientation. Just like a compass it provides direction for the pilgrim. Just like a compass it makes straight the crooked roads of life. But just like a compass, we need to know how to use it. We need to know how to interpret it.

The basic question of Bible interpretation is, "What is its purpose?"

Why is it important to know the purpose of the Bible?

Imagine your reaction if I were to take a telephone book, open it up, and proclaim, "I have found a list of everyone who's on welfare!" Or "Here is a list of college graduates!" Or, "This book will tell us who has a red car." You'd probably say, "Now wait a minute—that's not the purpose of that book. You're holding a telephone book. Its purpose is simply to reveal the name and number of residents of a city during a certain time frame."

Only by understanding its purpose can I accurately use the telephone book. Only by understanding its purpose can I accurately use the Bible. By assuming the Bible has some other purpose, people have made some false assumptions and inaccurate applications. For example, some have assumed that the purpose of the Bible is to transplant the dress and food from first-century culture to today. Certain religions go into great detail about clothing and customs, assuming that is the goal of God and the Bible.

Some believe the Bible provides the student with a secret code of prophecy which, once deciphered, will reveal the day on which our Lord will return. Others believe the Bible is a secret success manual for wealth and health. Still others use the Bible to substantiate already-held beliefs. Some Christians feel the purpose of the Bible is to provide a pattern for the organization of the New Testament church. Though the Bible may have thoughts on each of these subjects, none of them identifies the purpose of Scripture. What is the purpose of the Bible? Let the Bible itself answer that question.

PART 1:
FOLLOW-ALONG NOTES

USE THIS WORKSHEET AS YOU LISTEN TO "HOW TO STUDY THE BIBLE, PART 2."

Many people believe the Bible is a compass of life. Many others scoff at such claims. What do you believe about the Bible?

The Bible is a remarkable book in _____. The Bible

   has one central theme: _____.

The Bible is a remarkable book in _____. The Bible tells it all!

The Bible is remarkable in its _____. Many have tried
   to extinguish the Bible but have failed.

The Bible is remarkable in its _____. The Bible is
   more than just another book.

HOW DO WE KNOW THE BIBLE IS TRUE?

LUKE 24:25–27

EXTERNAL EVIDENCE

1. Can it pass the test of _____?

2. Can it pass the _____ test?

3. Can it pass the _____ test?

4. Can it pass the test of _____?

INTERNAL EVIDENCE

1. The voice of the _____.

2. The voice of _____   _____.

3. The voice of the _____   _____.

If you do not accept the Bible, what is your Plan B?

PART 2:
GOING DEEPER

PERSONAL STUDY AND REFLECTION

• According to the following passages of Scripture, what is the purpose of the Bible?

2 Timothy 3:15:

_____

_____

_____

John 20:31:

_____

_____

_____

Romans 1:16–17:

_____

_____

_____

- *The purpose of the Bible is simply to proclaim God's plan to save His children. It asserts that man is lost and needs to be saved. And it communicates the message that Jesus is God in the flesh sent to save His children.*

How does the purpose of the Bible affect the message of the Bible?

_____

_____

_____

_____

- Describe a situation in your life in which the Bible clearly told you what decision you should make. What did you do? How did the situation turn out?

_____

_____

_____

_____

- Describe a situation in which the Scriptures were not as clear. What did you do? How did the situation turn out?

_____

_____

_____

_____

- *The philosophy of man is ever-changing. There was a time when the common belief was that the world was flat. We now know that's not true. Today, the so-called wise teachers of science declare emphatically that man evolved from apes, and before that from microbes in the ocean. But this assertion contradicts the very science that these people hold to so religiously—there is simply no evidence on which to base a claim.*

The textbooks that we used in science class when I was in elementary school would be laughed at today because we have discovered so many new things that we didn't understand then. Imagine what children in fifty years will say about the things that "wise" man hold as fact today. The truth is that God has created such a complex universe, and there are so many new discoveries today that scientists are coming to the realization that man's understanding of the world around him is imperfect, and will always be so.

But there is one thing in this world that is never changing, and that is God's Word.

- Read 1 Corinthians 3:18–21. How does God see the wisdom of the world?

_____

_____

- Read 1 Corinthians 2:6–16. How are the things of God revealed to us?

_____

_____

- Whose mind do we have which enables us to understand the things of God?

_____

_____

- *It is the truly wise person who builds his life on the rock of God's Word!*

  The Bible was written over the span of some 1,500 years by forty different writers. These men and women lived centuries apart, in different areas of the ancient Middle East. The background of these people varied greatly from shepherds and fishermen, to doctors, lawyers, and kings. Parts of the Bible were written in three different languages: Hebrew, Greek, and Aramaic. There was no way for these people to gather and discuss what was being added to the Bible— it had to have been compiled under the divine direction of the Holy Spirit.

How trustworthy does the Bible seem to you? Explain your answer.

_____

_____

_____

_____

_____

_____

Though the Bible was written over sixteen centuries by at least forty authors, it has one central theme—salvation through faith in Christ. Begun by Moses in the lonely desert of Arabia and finished by John on the lonely Isle of Patmos, it is held together by a strong thread: God's passion and God's plan to save His children. What a vital truth! Understanding the purpose of the Bible is like setting the compass in the right direction. Calibrate it correctly and you'll journey safely. But fail to set it, and who knows where you'll end up. ■

*Reading the Bible
without meditating
on it is like trying to eat
without swallowing.*

ANONYMOUS

LESSON THREE:

INTERPRETING THE BIBLE

*Do your best to present yourself
to God as one approved, a workman who
does not need to be ashamed and
who correctly handles the word of truth.*

2 TIMOTHY 2:15

OVERVIEW

Some time ago I sat down with my daughters to play a card game. We had received the game several months ago and remembered the fun we had the first time we tried it. So we decided to play again.

The cards were not the typical ones with spades and aces, but rather a different set designed especially for this contest. As we dealt the cards, we realized something was missing—the instructions. We couldn't find the instructions.

No problem, we thought. We'll remember the rules as we go along.

One of the girls asked how a person wins this game. We couldn't remember. That was also on the instruction sheet. No problem, we thought. We'll figure out the goal as we go along.

The results were interesting. First, we tended to make up rules which fit our personal needs. (Amazing how a bad draw can jar your memory about an obscure rule offering second chances.)

Since we couldn't remember how to determine the winner, we all had different objectives. Some wanted to amass as many cards as possible. Others wanted to lose as many cards as possible. Since we didn't know the objective, we couldn't agree on the plan.

The result was chaos. Four people making four sets of rules with four different objectives. Fortunately, we finally found the instructions and learned, to the surprise of each of us, that none of us was entirely correct.

It's hard to play together if you don't know the goal.

Now take that simple card game and amplify it by two millenniums of heritage and centuries of denominational loyalty and a dozen or so layers of religious tradition and you have an idea as to the difficulty of biblical interpretation.

Students of Scripture need to ask the same question we asked at the card game, "What did the designer have in mind?" What is God's goal in Scripture? And, what are His rules of interpretation? Focus on these questions and you'll clarify your study. For that reason, we need to be careful about using the right rules of interpretation.

PART 1:
FOLLOW-ALONG NOTES

USE THIS WORKSHEET AS YOU LISTEN TO "HOW TO STUDY THE BIBLE, PART 3."

- If we have any understanding at all of God's Word, it's because of the Holy Spirit. (John 14:26)

- It is necessary for the student to want to learn. (Psalm 119:167)

RULES OF INTERPRETATION

- What is the purpose of the Bible? To reveal God's _____ and

  _____ for salvation.

  - 2 Timothy 3:15
  - Romans 1:16–17
  - John 20:31

• Why is it important to understand the purpose of the Bible? The task of

the student is _____.

TOOLS OF INTERPRETATION

1. The Test of _____: How vital is this point to the
   theme of the Bible?

     • 1 Corinthians 15:3–5
     • 2 Timothy 2:8
     • Matthew 23:23

2. The Test of _____: Does this point transcend
   cultural eras and situational particulars?

3. The Test of _____: What was the original intent
   of the author when he picked up the pen?

4. The Test of _____: What does the Bible really say?

5. The Test of _____: What personal biases do I
   bring to the text?

PART 2:
GOING DEEPER

PERSONAL STUDY AND REFLECTION

NOTE: SENTENCES IN ITALICS ARE DIRECTLY FROM MAX'S AUDIO LESSON.

Let's take a look at some different rules of interpretation of the Bible.

1. The Test of Priority

This test holds that there are some sections of Scripture that possess more compelling relevance to the human condition than others.

- What do Paul's words in 1 Corinthians 15:3–5 have to do with the test of priority?

_____

_____

_____

• What are the truths that Paul states are the "most important"?

_____

_____

• *The Bible is not a flat landscape void of mountain peaks and highlands. It has great variety in contour and geography. Though every word of the Bible is important, not every word is equally important Though every text contributes to the whole, not every text is of equal weight. For example, the same apostle Paul spoke regarding the resurrection of Christ and the jewelry of women. Are the topics of equal importance? Hardly. We can disagree regarding clothing, but to disagree regarding the resurrection could prove fatal. The good Bible student majors in the majors and minors in the minors.*

Jesus criticized the religious leaders of His day for not doing this. Summarize His words found in Matthew 23:23.

_____

_____

· Is it possible to know the Bible and miss its central message? Why or why not?

_____

_____

2. The Test of Consistency

Truths that matter tend to resurface regardless of culture or era. Regardless of nation or century. Biblical teaching regarding decency and humility is consistent. The principle of tolerance and unity threads its way throughout the Bible. Ask yourself, "Was this statement intended to be a permanent rule or was it a specific instruction given to address a specific situation?" Give it the test of consistency.

Let's pause and consider two examples of this on contemporary controversial issues: the role of women in the church and the practice of homosexuality.

· Read 1 Timothy 2:11–12 and 1 Corinthians 14:34–35. What was Paul's instruction regarding the women's role concerning the men in the church?

_____

_____

- Were these statements intended to become a permanent rule or were they a specific command given by Paul to a specific situation? What do you think?

  _____

  _____

  _____

- *Let's give it the test of consistency. Did Paul teach the same in other cities and write the same in other letters? It might surprise you to know that he did not.*

  Read Romans 16:1. What woman's name is listed as a deacon in the church? In Romans 16:3, what woman is listed as an apostle?

  _____

- Now read Acts 18:26, Acts 21:9, and 1 Corinthians 11:5. According to these verses, what were women allowed to do in these churches?

  _____

· Why would Paul allow women to speak in one church but not in another? What do you think?

_____

_____

_____

· *A careful study of 1 Timothy reveals that troublesome women were a major part of the problem at the church. Apparently the problem in Ephesus was a local problem. And the instructions regarding silence were intended for those listeners.*

What does the Bible teach about homosexuality? Can you back up your answer with Scripture passages?

_____

_____

_____

- *Some suggest that the Bible's teachings against homosexuality are culturally relative and do not apply today. Throughout the Bible, however, homosexuality is consistently considered wrong. The command transcends historical particularity. Nowhere in the Old or New Testaments does the Bible endorse homosexual activity. Not in one single verse. Eight passages condemn it outright. And these denouncements are not limited to one era or locale. As early as the book of Leviticus and as late as the letters to Corinth and Rome, homosexuality is presented as a sin.*

Sound Bible study includes a search for the recurring themes of the Bible. Truths that matter tend to resurface regardless of culture or era. Regardless of nation or century. Note how the Master Teacher used all of the Bible when He taught.

Read Luke 24:25–27. Where did Jesus turn for His message to the people?

_____

_____

_____

_____

· What meaning could this have for you today?

_____

_____

_____

· *As we study, we should do the same. Study the Bible. As you do, pursue the recurring themes of Scripture. In so doing, you will understand what matters to God.*

What difference will learning the rules of Bible interpretation have on your personal study of God's Word?

_____

_____

_____

_____

· What has God taught you through His Word lately?

_____

_____

_____

_____

· What changes are you making in your life based on what He has taught you?

_____

_____

_____

_____

*Nobody ever
outgrows Scripture;
the book widens
and deepens
with our years.*

CHARLES SPURGEON

LESSON FOUR:

READ THE STORY!

For the word of God is living and active,
sharper than any two-edged sword,
piercing to the division of soul and of spirit,
of joints and of marrow, and discerning
the thoughts and intentions of the heart.

HEBREWS 4:12

OVERVIEW

Are you studying the Bible for yourself? Or are you letting others interpret the Bible for you?

"The man who looks into the perfect law... and makes a habit of so doing, is not the man who hears and forgets. He puts that law into practice and he wins true happiness" (James 1:25 Phillips).

Imagine you are selecting your food from a cafeteria line. You pick your salad, you choose your entrée, but when you get to the vegetables, you see a pan of something that turns your stomach.

"Yuck! What's this?" you ask, pointing.

"Oh, you don't want to know," replies a slightly embarrassed server.

"Yes, I do."

"Well, if you must. It's a pan of pre-chewed food."

"What?"

"Pre-chewed food. Some people prefer to swallow what others have chewed."

Repulsive? You bet. But widespread. More so than you might imagine. Not with cafeteria food, but with God's Word.

Such Christians mean well. They even listen well. But they discern little. They are content to swallow whatever they are told. No wonder they've stopped growing. Remember: "Be careful in your life and in your teaching" (1 Timothy 4:16).

PART 1:
FOLLOW-ALONG NOTES

USE THIS WORKSHEET AS YOU LISTEN TO "HOW TO STUDY THE BIBLE, PART 4."

- The question is not how to find a Bible, but how to apply the Bible.

  (Nehemiah 8:1–12)

- The people _____ the Book.

- The people _____ the Book.

  The greatest way we can respect the Bible is to use it the way it was intended to be used.

- The teachers _____ the Book.

3 IMPORTANT WORDS

_____: God revealing His truth to man

_____: Inspired writers receiving and recording the truth

_____: God's people understanding and applying the truth

• The people _____ to the Book.

PART 2:
GOING DEEPER

PERSONAL STUDY AND REFLECTION

NOTE: SENTENCES IN ITALICS ARE DIRECTLY FROM MAX'S AUDIO LESSON.

Read the story.

When life closes in, read the story. When someone you trusted repays you with dishonesty, read the story.

When searing yesterdays stall soaring todays, read the story.

When you've been knocked off the mountaintop and climbing back up seems hopeless, read the story.

You're faced with a decision. What do you do with your disillusionment? What do you do with your broken heart? We're not talking inconveniences or hassles. We're not discussing long lines or red lights or a bad game of tennis. We're talking heartbreak. What do you do with that heartbreak? Read the story.

That's what Jesus did when He encountered two disillusioned followers on the road from Jerusalem to Emmaus, a couple of days after His death.

Read Luke 24:13–35.

· Who was going to Emmaus and what were the two men discussing along the way?

_____

_____

· Who appeared to the men on the way to Emmaus?

_____

· What emotions did the two men display?

_____

· How had the events of the last few days crushed the expectations of the two men talking with Jesus?

_____

_____

· Why did Jesus explain the Scriptures to the men?

_____

_____

· *Notice what Jesus did: He told them the story! Not just any story. He told them the story of God and God's plan for the people. Read Luke 24:27. It's fascinating that Jesus' cure for the broken heart is the story of God. He started with Moses and finished with Himself. Why did He do that? Why did He retell the ancient tale? Because what they heard is what we all need to hear when we are disappointed:*

We need to hear that God is still in control. We need to hear that it's not over until He says so. The way to deal with discouragement? The cure for disappointment? Go back to the story. Read it again and again. Read the story, and remember, their story is yours!

- According to Luke 24:33-35, how did these men respond to their encounter with Jesus?

_____

- How does reading the story of God's Word cause you to respond?

_____

_____

_____

The challenge too great? Read the story.

That's you crossing the Red Sea with Moses.

Too many worries? Read the story.

That's you receiving heavenly food with the Israelites.

Your wounds too deep? Read the story.

That's you, Joseph, forgiving your brothers for betraying you.

Your enemies too mighty? Read the story.

That's you marching with Jehoshaphat into a battle already won.

Your disappointments too heavy? Read the story of the Emmaus-bound disciples.

The Savior they thought was dead now walked beside them. He entered their house and sat at their table. And something happened in their hearts.

• Read Luke 24:31. What happened to the disciples who heard the Word as Jesus explained it to them?

_____

_____

• Is there a time when God's Word helped you through a difficult situation?

_____

_____

_____

· How might the Word help you through a difficult situation in the future?

_____

_____

The next time you're disappointed, don't panic. Don't bail out. Don't give up. Just be patient. Return to the Word, and let God remind you He's still in control.

Read the story!

PROMISES FROM BECOMING A STUDENT OF GOD'S WORD

Savor the following promises that God gives to those who determine to become a student of His Word. One way that you can carry the message of this study with you everywhere in your heart is through the lost art of memorization. Select a couple of the verses below to commit to memory.

I have hidden your word in my heart
that I might not sin against you.

PSALM 119:11

Your word is a lamp to my feet
and a light for my path.

PSALM 119:105

Man does not live on bread alone but on every
word that comes from the mouth of the LORD.

DEUTERONOMY 8:3B

*All Scripture is God-breathed and is useful for teaching,
rebuking, correcting and training in righteousness, so that the man
of God may be thoroughly equipped for every good work.*

2 TIMOTHY 3:16-17

Oh, how I love your law! I meditate on it all day long.

PSALM 119:97

SUGGESTIONS FOR MEMBERS OF A GROUP STUDY

The Bible says that we should not forsake the assembling of ourselves together (see Hebrews 10:25). A small-group Bible study is one of the best ways to grow in your faith. As you meet together with other people, you will discover new truths about God's Word and challenge one another to greater levels of faith. The following are suggestions for you to get the most out of a small-group study of this material.

1. Come to the study prepared. Follow the suggestions for individual study mentioned previously. You will find that careful preparation will greatly enrich your time spent in group discussion.

2. Be willing to participate in the discussion. The leader of your group will not be lecturing. Instead, he or she will be encouraging the members of the group to discuss what they have learned. The leader will be asking the questions that are found in this guide.

3. Stick to the topic being discussed.

4. Be sensitive to the other members of the group. Listen attentively when they describe what they have learned. You may be surprised by their insights! Many questions do not have "right" answers, particularly questions that aim at meaning or application. Instead the questions push us to explore the passage more thoroughly.

5. When possible, link what you say to the comments of others. Also be affirming whenever you can. This will encourage some of the more hesitant members of the group to participate.

6. Expect God to teach you through the passage being discussed and through the other members of the group. Pray that you will have an enjoyable and profitable time together, but also that as a result of this study, you will find ways that you can take action individually and/or as a group.

7. Remember that anything said in the group is considered confidential and should not be discussed outside the group unless specific permission is given to do so.

LEADER'S GUIDE

LESSON ONE: A MOST PECULIAR BOOK

1. Begin the session with prayer. Ask God to be with you as you begin to study His Word together.

2. Play the audio segment of the CD entitled "How to Study the Bible, Part 1." Encourage group members to take notes in the section of their study guide entitled "Follow-Along Notes."

3. Begin group discussion by asking the following questions. Allow each group member ample time to answer, if they desire to do so.

   - Has there ever been a time when reading the Scriptures helped you through a difficult time in your life? Explain.

   - Has there ever been a time when reading the Scriptures has been difficult for you to do? Why or why not?

   - Read Matthew 7:7. How can the principles of "ask, seek, and knock" be applied to the study of God's Word?

   - How have you followed these three steps in your own Bible study? What was the result?

- According to James 1:25, what is the reward for choosing to learn and obey God's Word? How have you seen this reward in your own life?

4. Remind everyone to complete the "Going Deeper: Personal Study and Reflection" section for lesson two before the next group session.

5. Be sure to close in prayer. Invite the group participants to share prayer requests with the group and encourage them to pray for one another.

LESSON TWO: THE PURPOSE OF THE BIBLE

1. Begin the session with prayer. Ask God to be with you as you begin to study His Word together.

2. Play the audio segment of the CD entitled "How to Study the Bible, Part 2." Encourage group members to take notes in the section of their study guide entitled "Follow-Along Notes."

3. Begin group discussion by asking the following questions. Allow each group member ample time to answer, if they desire to do so.

- What do you believe the purpose of the Bible to be? Why is it important to read the Bible with this purpose in mind?

- Have you ever known someone to try to use the Bible for a different purpose than what it was intended? What was the result?

- Have you ever considered the evidence, both external and internal, that the Bible is true? How does this evidence strengthen your faith?

- Describe a situation in your life in which the Bible told you what decision you should make. What did you do? How did the situation turn out?

- Describe a situation in which the Scriptures were not as clear. What did you do? How did the situation turn out?

- How trustworthy does the Bible seem to you? Explain your answer.

4. Remind everyone to complete the "Going Deeper: Personal Study and Reflection" section for lesson three before the next group session.

5. Be sure to close in prayer. Invite the group participants to share prayer requests with the group and encourage them to pray for one another.

LESSON THREE: INTERPRETING THE BIBLE

1. Begin the session with prayer. Ask God to be with you as you begin to study His Word together.

2. Play the audio segment of the CD entitled "How to Study the Bible, Part 3." Encourage group members to take notes in the section of their study guide entitled "Follow-Along Notes."

3. Begin group discussion by asking the following questions. Allow each group member ample time to answer, if they desire to do so.

- What challenges do you see in interpreting the Bible? Why is it important to understand the purpose of the Bible when interpreting it?

- Which tool of interpretation seems the simplest to you? Which seems more difficult? Why?

- How can the interpretation of the Bible affect a Christian's response to the cultural issues of our day?

- In what ways has your own personal interpretation of the Bible affected your response to the cultural issues of our day?

- How can you become a better student of God's Word?

4. Remind everyone to complete the "Going Deeper: Personal Study and Reflection" section for lesson four before the next group session.

5. Be sure to close in prayer. Invite the group participants to share prayer requests with the group and encourage them to pray for one another.

LESSON FOUR: READ THE STORY!

1. Begin the session with prayer. Ask God to be with you as you begin to study His Word together.

2. Play the audio segment of the CD entitled "How to Study the Bible, Part 4." Encourage group members to take notes in the section of their study guide entitled "Follow-Along Notes."

3. Begin group discussion by asking the following questions. Allow each group member ample time to answer, if they desire to do so.

- How did the people in Nehemiah's day respect the Word of God? How do you respect God's Word today?

- Read Luke 24:31. What happened to the disciples who heard the Word as Jesus explained it to them? How can you apply this to your own life today?

- What has God taught you through His Word lately?

- What changes are you making in your life based on what He has taught you?

4. Be sure to close in prayer. Invite the group participants to share prayer requests with the group and encourage them to pray for one another.

MAX LUCADO'S

MAX on life

S E R I E S

AVAILABLE WHEREVER BOOKS ARE SOLD.